Finding Healing

at the End of Arrogance

Stories and Reflections Based on

A Course In Miracles

Liliana Bejarano

ISBN-13: 978-1974034161
ISBN-10:197403416X

Illustrations pixabay.com under Creative Commons Deed CC0.

Spanish Version: Sanación al Final de la arrogancia.

Liliana Bejarano

www.miraclencounters.com

miraclencounters@gmail.com

DEDICATION

To my beloved husband for his unconditional support, to my parents and sisters who became my first teachers, and whose unconditional love encourages me to advance in my journey.

To all who feel what is truly important in their lives goes beyond what they can perceive with their senses. To those whom resist the belief they are victims of the chaotic universe they experience, and to those whom, in a corner of their being are certain that happiness is something inherent in their creation. And for all those who know there must be another way of seeing the world.

CONTENTS

ACKNOWLEDGMENTS

To those who believed in this project and generously participated in the process of editing and graphic concept: Hector Cañón Spanish editing, my husband Tony Cryer for the translation from the Spanish version and Ray Commeau for his help with the editing of the English version. To all those who crossed my life, if only briefly, and unwittingly inspired the stories and reflections of this book.

In you is all of Heaven. Every leaf that falls is given life in you. Each bird that ever sang will sing again in you. And every flower that ever bloomed has saved its perfume and its loveliness for you. (ACIM)

INTRODUCTION

My journey started long ago, when I came to a point in my life where the pain began to be unbearable and I decided I could no longer live with it. The space surrounding me had become very small and the air too heavy. One of us had to go, either the pain or I would have to leave.

I packed its bags and threw them off a balcony, shouting ferociously that I would not have it in my life any longer. I remember it turned its pale face towards me, gave me a wink, and with a sigh of relief, the pain left.

My uncompromising decision came along the same day I asked for help. This was presented to me in the form of an enigmatic blue book. Since that moment, a burst of light began to crack the walls of the prison I had built around myself. When the light could not contain itself any longer, there was an explosion which was felt to the ends of the universe. The light had destroyed my prison, and there I was in the midst of the debris, wiping the ashes from my eyes, truly seeing for the very first time.

I found that all my life I had only been hurting myself. I had been prey to my own thoughts. It was only my mind that needed to be healed.

I needed a new thought system, one in which all my resentments, guilt and fears could vanish. Gradually I understood the true meaning of forgiveness, and the freedom that would follow. This blue book with gold lettering and the unusual title, A Course in Miracles, showed me that I could find healing through forgiveness, only if stopped being arrogant.

When I stopped being arrogant, I stopped trying to tell God how to act, what to give me and how to serve me.

When I stopped being arrogant, I also stopped believing that I was always right and recognized the joy being wrong.

When I stopped being arrogant, I also stopped drinking the poison of my own judgments. I relinquished the proud role of playing the victim.

I realized that I cannot change anyone else. No one has to change in order for me to be happy. The only one who had to change was me.

I stopped thinking that I could have created a self other than the one God created and began to accept His will for me is perfect happiness.

When we stop being arrogant, we can be still and listen to what He has to tell us.

God speaks to us in the form of experiences; some of which are narrated in the book as reflections and stories. Most of the reflections are questions I asked myself and tried to answer; however, they will only make sense to you as you try to find the answers for yourself; when you are in silence and listen to what infinite wisdom has to tell you. The Stories of Forgiveness, are based on true stories of people I have encountered over the years, who have made an impact in my life for their courage to overcome any challenge through the healing power of forgiveness.

Take this book and open it when you need help. Read a reflection or story and meditate on it, keep an open mind, and when you go through a difficult period, always remember that "This need not be" ACIM.

There is always another way to see everything!

Author's Note: Throughout the book I kept the same language I used in the Spanish original, which is also found in A Course In Miracles, which uses a male distinction for God. I have come to respect and embrace the many different expressions of our divine source. In recent years I have moved from the concept of God as a male figure to a more universal, non gender one, God as the ultimate source of love, perfection and infinite wisdom in the universe, and in my life.

How deep is the bottom?

Dispirited, you wonder, "What did I do to deserve this?" You quietly contemplate the crushing scenario, and in the distance are the "guilty ones," who lie camouflaged and ready to strike at you with their insatiable rage.

All around you is a potential enemy. You walk through a minefield, in a world where you must defend yourself against injustices, where you have to fight and sacrifice to achieve your dreams. You persist in an ambitious and desperate race for happiness, bitterly proving the futility of all your sacrifice.

Pretentious happiness is very slippery, it is intended only for the lucky, the strong, the wealthy, the proud, for anyone except you.

Happiness shows you its face for just a few seconds only to smile at you with disdain. It is elusive. It is spoiled. You cannot look at it closely and you cannot possess it. You saw its ethereal face when you got that late model car. It also gave you a hint when you received that degree you wanted. It gave you a slightly more serious nod when your son was born, when you got married, when you built your dream home; but then it turned its face and mocked you once again as everything disappeared before your inconsolable tears Everything failed you. Everything faded.

You have fallen, but how deep is the bottom for you? How much tolerance do you have for pain? Everything indicates that you are happily stuck in a cycle of self abuse that you repeat over and over again.

If you are addicted to suffering you will never have enough misery. You will find scenarios that will bring you heavy doses of fear and pain. You will create the characters and conflicts needed to satisfy your addiction momentarily. Eagerly you will look for the guilty ones and the enemies outside, when your only enemy is yourself.

You cannot find happiness simply because you are not looking for it. True happiness neither hides nor mocks you. It can be found in the only place where you had forgotten to look, inside you. You had endeavored to search for it along the road to hell and down there, of course, you could never find it.

Happiness is a permanent state. It is the loss of fear. It is the experience you have when you live in the healing power of forgiveness. It is your inheritance, the decision which lies at your fingertips at all times. You can now decide that you have finally touched the bottom of your devastation and dare to ask for something new.

You have only suffered from your thoughts, and only because you are stuck in a past or future that does not exist. Inside of you resides all the power to reverse the thought system with which you attacked yourself and realize that you were the one responsible for your downfall.

When will you decide how deep is your bottom? It depends entirely on you. At any time you can decide enough is enough, and when you do it genuinely, all the miracles will be given you. That is the moment when you finally find the peace you desire.

Ask for help. You are not alone.

.

What if everything was just a dream?

It is estimated that there are as many galaxies as grains of sand on the planet. Ours, the Milky Way, is one of them. It contains about 400 billion of stars. One of these stars is our Sun. It is tiny in size compared to its neighbors. This little Sun has a system of eight planets, including one called Earth which could fit inside the Sun 1,300,000 times.

That is where we live. We name this small planet "The World," and we consider it to be all that exists. Our few years of life on it seem endless, and we consider every experience a tragic comedy that crazy fate forces us to live.

We look at the infinite universe as if it were a vague idea in the imagination of a deranged poet, blurred, unreal, with no relevance to what we perceive with our senses as tangible and real.

We live a modest 70 or 80 years in a universe that is

almost fourteen billion years old. Still, few have dared to question what happens in the remainder of time.

Why all this time, and why the existence of many galaxies if what we call "our life" relates only to those 80 turns that this planet makes around the Sun? Why would the creator of the universe become tired of living those billions of years in peace and then decide to conceive a human race just to torment itself, watching them destroy each other and then punish them for the rest of eternity?

If this doesn't make any sense to you then you can dare to search for a different answer, which will present itself to you through an experience.

If you take the risk, you might discover that you also are part of that infinite and eternal universe. You are connected perfectly to everything because you were created by the same divine source. A source that is the extraordinary expression of perfection and love. A source that can have no opposite for It is all there is. A source that connects us with everything. If you were created by the eternal, you are also eternal, not in your physical identity, but in your true essence.

We are being constantly deceived by our senses. We see an apparent movement of the Sun when it is really the earth that revolves around it. We seem to be walking on a flat surface, when it is actually curved and the thousands of stars we see in the sky were extinct millions of years ago. Still, we give much credence to what our senses perceive. What if we found out that what we call reality is just a dream, an illusion?

We value everything we see because we want to see it. What if one day we would accept responsibility

17

for what we see around us and recognize that everything only obeyed our wishes, our desires to live in calamity, in lack, or in abundance. We decide to live in greed or in generosity, in love or in the clutches of a sordid resentment.

Once we are determined to see something new, we will see it. Our lives would change. When we give up our drama and addictions, when we recognize that attacking someone else is an attack on ourselves; that is the moment we can leave the suffocating weight of our past and begin to see the present. Now we will be able to see beyond the veil all of our ideas, judgments and blame, and find that what we gave so much importance was completely insignificant.

Would you be willing to accept that your life can change the moment you change your mind? All you see is part of a dream from which you can awaken any time you want. We will see things differently when we remember the entire universe is within us.

There is nothing to fear. The recognition of this is the miracle of our awakening.

Forgiveness is the key to happiness.

Here is the answer to your search for peace. Here is the key to meaning in a world that seems to make no sense. Here is the way to safety in apparent dangers that appear to threaten you at every turn, and bring uncertainty to all your hopes of ever finding quietness and peace. Here are all questions answered; here the end of all uncertainty ensured at last. (ACIM)

What is forgiveness?

It's one of those questions that seems easy to answer until you try, so let's start with what it is not.

Forgiveness is not giving consent to the world to run all over us again and again, enduring the miseries "in the name of love." This could be the case with the woman who allows her drunken husband to hit her every weekend and then "forgives him," only with the certainty that he will do it again. This is just tolerance of a sick and abusive situation. It has nothing to do with the true meaning of forgiveness. To forgive is to release what is killing us.

By forgiving we don't give reward to an abusive party. If we think so, we will begin to evaluate whether it is deserved or not to give it and thus have a justification to continue feeding our resentments.

Here is an example.

For three years Daniela worked as a secretary in a small company that was emerging from a major crisis. Leonora, the CEO, deeply trusted her because she was the daughter of one of her former employees whom she held dear. After the company had two difficult years, the CEO decided it was the time to review the financial records. Very soon, the new accountant discovered Daniela had been embezzling thousands of dollars over the past year. Beyond the thousands lost, Leonora had difficulty accepting the betrayal. What hurt the most was to think that her trust had been broken. For a long time, she kept remembering the events with anger and mortification at the ingenuity of the act. She fired Daniela but couldn't forgive her because she thought doing so would give her a reward for her betrayal, and she was far from deserving it.

Forgiveness is not to reward for those who do not deserve it. Forgiveness is an act of self-love.

When you love yourself, you stop attacking yourself. The road then becomes clear in your mind, and you can discern what hurts you and what gives you peace. Releasing resentments will become a natural act, and forgiveness will appear as a healing glow in which the shadows of the past fade away. If you love yourself, you will have enough strength to abandon everything that interferes with your peace.

In the case of the woman beaten by her drunken husband, forgiveness will begin with an act of love for herself, and she will seek for help. She will move out or notify the authorities to prevent further contact with her attacker. That decision has to be uncompromising. She may suggest a support group for him to treat his alcoholism; but whether he accepts or not, she can enter into a program for co-dependents. The opportunities are endless. Meanwhile, her inner clearing will begin. First by forgiving herself for having accepted the abuse in her life and second, to accept what happened as an opportunity to get rid of her desire to live in suffering. She will be able to forgive her husband without disturbing the peace she already chose for her life. When she gives no more value to suffering, it will begin to fade.

For Leonora, her healing will come when she discovers that forgiveness is not an award for her former secretary, but for herself. It is to give herself the gift of a serene mind.

Forgiveness is not for anyone else, forgiveness is for yourself. It is an inner cleansing, a bath of light that will erase all the sorrows of your mind and restore your peace. You just need the will to do it, here and now.

What would you do if you had no fear?

A while ago I saw a commercial on the internet with an open question: "What would you do if you had no fear?" Images of a woman were shown, who since childhood, had been very fearful of different scenarios such as: walking into the ocean, public speaking, approaching a boy she liked, giving her opinion at work meetings. The next morning I asked the same question to my colleagues. "What would you do if you had no fear?"

"It would be wonderful," said one of them, with an air of nostalgia.

"That would be very arrogant," objected another.

Perhaps you have been persuaded about the "value" of fear from a very young age. You have been told that it is necessary to prevent you from performing acts that endanger your safety or the safety of those around you. But do you really think that fear is protecting something worthwhile? You have made up your human identity out of fears which are vehemently justified. You are afraid to express yourself, afraid to talk to your boss, of being alone, of aging, of losing something you love. You are afraid to be free. In all cases you imagine completely devastating events and scenarios that are only in your imagination.

Fear is what makes you a prisoner of your thoughts, paralyzing you and making you lose all hope of finding the peace you deserve. It is fear that makes you live a mediocre life, doing work which you hate. Fear binds you to a partner with whom you have little in common, and also the reason you do not dare to venture out and see the world.

What are you actually afraid of? Are you afraid of death? What if you knew that your true Self is eternal. Would you still be afraid? What you think you are is not your true Self. Your body is just a temporary physical configuration, which is transcended by the real You.

What we are afraid of is life and love. We are fearful of being happy. In some corner of our being we know that by letting go of our fears we find our salvation and that scares us more than living a miserable life.

A life in fear cannot offer anything useful to you. Instead, it makes you a prisoner in your own mind.

The commercial I mentioned at the beginning of this story ends when the main character has a face to face encounter in the woods with a threatening wolf. She jumps on him with all the courage and adrenaline in her body, as she mentally performs every act which fear made impossible. She and the wolf pass through each other and finally the animal disappears.

Freedom from fear is something we can achieve when we recognize that we have a higher power that is in us, yet not from us, but available to us any time we decide to use it.

Anxiety

How many times have you seen a change in your body temperature or an alteration of your pulse at the thought of a future event that may never happen? Perhaps you live in a permanent restlessness, and all you crave is to smoke, drink or eat, in order to stop these uncontrollable anxiety attacks. However, when you calm your anxiety in that way, eventually you will feel worse because that feeling will be replaced by even stronger feelings of guilt.

Now observe yourself for an instant.

Watch your mind.

If you are experiencing anxiety it is because you are not living in the present moment. Your current thought system makes you create a future that is only in your imagination. It may be a reaction to your partner, boss, business, etc. These are all false ideas. All of them are recurrent images that are used to sabotage your inner peace..

Do you think it would be worthwhile to stop

investing your mental energy in those awkward scenarios and immerse yourself completely in the present moment? If so, dare to enter that unknown land of "The Now," the only moment that really exists.

Take a deep breath and watch the path of the air as it travels inside your body when you exhale.

Feel the air and light on your face, the temperature of the room, the presence of wellness in your home, the water on your skin, its texture.

Look around you, pick an object, listen to its silence and breathe.

If attack thoughts, defenses, or insanity comes to your mind, discard them. That is all.

If you can do it, it is because you are entering the Now. There all anxiety fades and you can live in the paradise of the present moment.

You can feel your stream of thoughts stop when you step into the now. Sedatives such as drugs, alcohol, smoking or overeating are not required any more.

Why do you think you will be abandoned or treated unfairly? Why do you always expect the worst case scenario? Allow an enormous sense of confidence to take you over, and remember that at all times you are being taking care of.

You are being supported in every instant. If you put your trust completely in the One who knows what is best for you, you will have nothing to fear. Anxiety and fear have no choice but to disappear.

*Sit quietly and close your eyes. The light within
you is sufficient. It alone has power to give the
gift of sight to you. Exclude the outer world,
and let your thoughts fly to the peace within.*
(ACIM)

Your Identity

Try to answer the question "Who am I?" without using a description based on your resume or profession; giving no details about your family, nationality or place of residence, without mentioning your age or your gender, with no reference to your degrees, past achievements or assets, without listing the qualities or defects that you think you have and without saying your name... Now, "Who are you?"

Maybe you are about to give up before you even start. In fact, finding this answer has been for centuries the goal of the spiritual quest of ascetics, Buddhists, shamans, Christians, Jews and Muslims, among others, as well as those who have dared to question their own perceptions, the ones who feel uncomfortable with suffering and of those who know that there is something else beyond what they can see.

Imagine for a moment that your whole identity is firmly rooted in being the employee of a company, but one day you are fired. Suppose that suddenly, one day you would lose all the things you use to describe yourself: your marriage, your children, your car, your house, even your country. What would you do? In an extreme case you might fall into a deep depression and try to commit suicide, or you may work hard to build a new identity that you feel suits you better. However, when you define yourself based on external factors, your whole life is an illusion. The bubble you make becomes a time bomb that will explode at any time and obliterate everything again.

Who you really are has nothing to do with the world around you, in fact, it has nothing to do with your possessions, nor what your visual perception shows you. Everything you see is perishable. If it is perishable it is not eternal. If is not eternal, is not real. Your true Self goes beyond what you can detect with your senses.

Inhale deeply and for an instant forget everything around you. Read carefully the following paragraph.

Still your mind and feel your breath. Imagine for a moment you can fly and look at yourself from a higher plane. Look at yourself while working, when you are with your family, or when you are angry. Remember that now you are seeing everything from "above the battlefield." In this way you will observe your emotions without being absorbed by them. You are a spectator. Although you think that character is you, it is not. It is assembled with the features you gave it, but it is not you. You can make that character perform a role of success or sacrifice. It will be what you want it to be because you made it up. Look into its heart and unleashed it. Beyond the cobwebs that you thought covered it, there is a light that cannot be contained. That light represents your true Self. Love is your essence and to offer it is your only function.

Cast aside the world of illusions you have made

only by being willing to make a shift in perception from fear to love ACIM.

Who needs to change?

Wanting everything around to change, so that we can live in a better world is perhaps not as noble an idea as we might think. We have invested a lot of energy, and we have slaughtered each other in the belief that humanity would be better off if there were just one race or one religion. We also torment ourselves daily as we gossip and criticize the behavior of our coworkers, neighbors and relatives. Somehow we believe that no one behaves the way they should.

When we judge, we disturb our own peace with the thought that everyone is wrong. Everyone must change to make this world better. Everyone but me.

A woman who had been married for fifteen years deeply believed her husband was the cause of all her misfortunes. Indeed, the man had lots of affairs and was also an obsessive gambler, which led him to be involved in several legal and financial problems. However, he had a good heart and was very responsible providing for his children who loved him unconditionally.

During the first years of marriage, the woman tried to attend some support groups for relatives of addicts and even tried psychotherapy. By now her constant depression had left her with a life full of bitterness. However, she soon gave up, explaining it was useless for her to continue therapy if the one who needed it was her husband. "He is the one who must attend," she insisted." Why do I need to change, if I am not an addict?"

She did not want to release her depression or her codependency. Perhaps it was more comfortable for her to remain in the victim roll than try to recognize her true one. For many years it was impossible for her to understand that the responsibility for improving her life was hers, not her husband's.

One day, after a tremendous altercation with one of her neighbors about a parking spot, that almost send them both to jail, she noticed that conflicts persisted around her, despite the distance of her partner. She was now struggling with all her relationships, even with her children and colleagues. In that moment, she finally realized that something was very wrong with her. If she could not continue to blame her husband for the hardships and problems still chasing her, it must be the cause of her distress was within her own mind. With her face wet with tears, she fell on her knees, and for first time she tasted the defeat of her own pride.

Asking for help was the only option she had never tried, and it was the only one that would get her out of hell. She started a healing therapy in which she gradually recognized her responsibility for her own misfortunes, and her deep need for forgiveness. She ceased to be defensive in every encounter with her loved ones, and she was happy to prove that if she changed her attitude, her environment would change as well.

She understood that her whole life was a projection of her mental state, and in her unconscious desire to remain a victim, she had thrown herself into an abyss. When she relinquished the idea of being a martyr and changed her mind about everything she saw, her life was renewed in a way she never imagined. She began to fully enjoy her family and friends. Disputes at work also ceased immediately. She stopped giving so much importance to little details, and a bright blue sky of optimism opened up for her. Now she had a calm mind and a thankful heart.

Who needs to change? The only one that needs to change is me.

Open your mind and receive all the gifts that God has given you. He did not send you into the world to suffer. Do not accept that as your reality because that is not Reality.

Rising from the shadows

Stories of forgiveness: Jacinto

Several years ago, while working in a small New England town, I met a remarkable man, who showed me the transforming power of forgiveness.

In this short and smiling, humble and hard-working man, you can see the peace in which he rests, after accomplishing a full day of work.

After collecting enough money to build his own mechanic shop, he longs to return to his country of origin in South America. He is very quiet, not because he does not like talking to people, but because he doesn't speak the language of the country he works in. In fact, he looks very pleased to speak with the few Hispanics at his work.

One day Jacinto and another co-worker named John sat next to me at lunchtime. During our conversation he learned John was recently married. He said to him, "You're very young, but you know what? At your age I was already married with five children."

At that moment his eyes clouded over a little, however, we could feel an air of tranquility in his words when he told us how he had lost his eldest son when he was only six years old. Although the pain was gone from his life, a bit of nostalgia was glimpsed in his soul. Nevertheless, he had no objection about telling us his history without us asking one single question.

"It was a summer day when my son and other children were playing at home. At that time, almost thirty years ago, we had no running water in the town where we lived. We had to store water in a small pool, which we covered with a tarp to avoid it becoming contaminated. The children were playing near the pool, when one of them pushed my son into the water and closed the tarp, thinking it was part of the game. When we arrived, we found his body floating."

For a second, which seemed like an eternity, my friend and I kept silent. Then in unison we let out a sigh, and for that instant, we could not understand, during such a tragic story, where his tranquility came from. Jacinto continued...

"In the following years I surrendered to alcohol. I smoked and drank every day until I lost consciousness. I did not realize that I was destroying myself and the rest of my family. One day, my wife, hurt by my behavior, said she would leave the house immediately with the children unless I stop drinking. Likewise, a priest who was a friend of the family spoke to me. He made me see that I could not do anything for my son, but I could do so many things for myself. Those were the words I heard and understood. More than 25 years have passed, and since then, I have not taken one drink. I love my children. Two of them are with me here, and we will return together to our country in a few months."

Jacinto holds no resentment towards the boy that pushed his son. He and his wife decided to consider everything as an accident, and rebuild their lives, concentrating on themselves and their other children.

Jacinto gets up from the table where he shares his story, smiles at us as usual; and singing songs of love, walks down the hall, saying a friendly goodbye, as a living demonstration of the healing power of forgiveness.

I watched, as the long line of regrets that had come between me and my happiness disappears before my eyes. The distance has collapsed and now this peace I discover within. In the place where I had never thought to look. ACIM

He leads me and knows the way, which I know not. Yet he will never keep from me what he would have me learn. And so I trust him to communicate to me all that he knows for me.

(ACIM)

What I see is what I think?

We can experience a lot of resistance when trying to accept the idea that everything that has happened in our lives has been with our consent. As a matter of fact, we might consider that idea to be outrageous. However, when we begin to identify some repeated stories in our life, we find some hints that tell us perhaps this thought might not be as absurd as we initially thought.

This was the case with Margaret.

Margaret's father was an alcoholic; her husband was an alcoholic, and so was her son, and with all of them, she lived through the worst abuse of her life. The woman was constantly complaining about every situation in her life. She used to highlight at all times the negative aspects of her work, family and society.

When her friends asked her about her view of life, she responded without haste; "Life is suffering, all you have to do is get used to the different forms it takes."

Would it be a coincidence that, in effect, she was living in the midst of a sea of suffering? She had accepted the pain as natural. All her actions and thoughts were focused on verifying this idea.

The world we see is a projection of our state of consciousness. When everything around us is chaotic it is because our minds are in chaos, it is because we are constantly cherishing thoughts of fear, sickness, revenge, resentment and guilt.

"I knew my wife would run off with another man. First, I lost my job, and now this. I knew it, I was right all along." says Santiago, whose pathological jealousy and infidelity had deteriorated his marriage and turned it into a battlefield. However, he wasn't able to see his participation in his own calamities.

In difficult situations, we tend to think life rages against us, when in fact, we are solely responsible for them. Unconsciously, we use situations, characters and patterns we have designed for ourselves to confirm our insane desire to always be right, our insane desire to suffer.

If we don't feel we deserve better, if we don't notice the love that is all around us, we will be attracted by conflict. We have attempted to solve our struggles by attacking and resisting whoever is around us; and as we all have experienced, those actions end up trapping us in more agony and more injustice.

Forgive yourself for the crazy pleasure you found by building up all that pain around you. Forgive yourself for believing devastation was natural, when in reality, what is natural is wellness and happiness. Forgive yourself for choosing hell instead of heaven, and then you will be ready to experience yourself as you really are, a magnificent expression of love itself.

Replace your thoughts of fear by letting the silence bring you thoughts of truth.

"Peace to my mind. Let all my thoughts be still." ACIM

To feel the Love of God within you is to see the world anew, shining in innocence, alive with hope, and blessed with perfect charity and love.
(*ACIM*)

Forgiving myself?

Some time ago, I was chatting with a friend who was struggling because of his past. His previous romantic relationships were a total disaster. He always ended up abandoning his partners when he thought he had found a better one. Despite this, he still proceeded in the same way; getting involved in dysfunctional relationships over and over again, and of course, no one came out unharmed.

I talked to him about the idea of self forgiveness, in order to start undoing the guilt, an idea that seemed quite puzzling to him. "If you forgive yourself, you will become a cold and merciless person," he replied.

For him self-forgiveness could foster cold blooded behavior, because any person would be able to harm humanity without regret. The absence of blame would make it easy for them to absolve themselves, thus they could live life without feeling the guilt, which he didn't believe was fair. Somehow he felt that guilt was needed in order to be a better human being. By feeling guilty he could redeem himself with the ones he had harmed and would thus avoid acting out atrocities in the future. If he was free of guilt he would be reduced to someone who was ruthless and unable to feel compassion for anyone. He held onto the guilt because he thought that this helped him become a better person.

But experience has shown us that no one who keeps feelings of sin and guilt could be in peace.

Guilt can only make us believe we are worthless and we deserve punishment. Over time, we will be trapped in devastating situations, fueled only by our own thoughts, and we will be unable to see where our adversities come from. To my friend, his deep need for punishment made his attraction to dysfunctional relationships very strong.

The truth is that blame is not the element that protects us from acting ruthlessly against anyone, love does. When we finally understand that by attacking someone else we attack ourselves, then we can stop it. The choice will be between hurting ourselves more or to start loving ourselves.

When you forgive yourself you can love unconditionally, you can embrace that innocent being within you. The idea of harming someone will be something that you will never consider. As you love yourself you will recognize yourself in the eyes of all those you behold, thus you will be able to love them as well.

Years later I was told that my friend, after going through a final devastating relationship, decided to ask for help and begin a process of self-forgiveness. He admitted, in his zeal to punish himself for his erratic behavior, he had been the creator of all his drama. Once he forgave himself, the cycle stopped. At that moment he realized he did not even need a partner to be at peace with himself. However, during that period of his life he found his life-partner, with whom he has lived ever since, sharing in a rich and happy relationship.

The greatest power that ever existed in the universe is the power of love, which is capable of inspiring the most extraordinary acts of forgiveness and healing. Its scope is not limited to time or space. It covers everything like a warm light that surrounds us and heals our wounds and our minds.

Releasing a thirty five year old burden of guilt.

Stories of forgiveness: Thomas
His testimony

The most guilt I think I ever felt, was the night my sweet friend, Angela, was raped by a stranger in California. We were on a High school field trip, we were both seventeen years old and I had a teenage crush on her. She was so sweet and tender with me always. I thought we might even begin a romance on this trip.

However, one night I left Angela alone at the local laundromat for about an hour. She was approached by a young man who offered to smoke a joint with her. Trustingly, she went off with the boy to the beach to get high. Once they were alone she became the victim of rape.

Upon my return I found the laundromat empty. The clothes she was washing were still in the machine. I quickly solicited the help of nearby security guards as well as all our friends. We frantically searched the entire neighborhood where we were staying, but she was nowhere to be found.

As our fear and trepidation grew, Angela suddenly appeared, crying, disheveled and obviously shaken. I knew at once what had occurred. Oh my God, I felt a terrible rage and awful guilt as well. If I had only stayed with her none of this would have happened. I felt totally responsible for her pain. I just wanted to find that guy, beat him within an inch of his life and put the bastard in a hospital for a good long time.

There was no forgiveness in me at all. I wanted to kill him if I could find him.

In the same week, the police captured a young man who fit the description of her assailant. The trial took place a few months later. His parents and lawyers managed to win the case and prevent the young man from being convicted by declaring no conclusive evidence was found, thus ending our hopes of justice, or so we thought. Perhaps justice comes in forms we cannot immediately recognize. I heard later this young man had turned his life around and learned a deep lesson in those three months he spent in jail. I doubt he ever attacked another human being for the rest of his life.

However, I carried the anger and guilt around with me for many years in the dark corners of my mind which I was afraid to visit. Here was this monster inside of me I knew existed, but tried to ignore. However, sometimes he appeared, and began tearing me apart when I least expected.

I saw Angela years later; she was married and had

moved on in her life, but I was still haunted by unforgiveness. Until one day I realized I was still assaulting myself with this memory. I had to do something.

What I did was a lesson from A Course in Miracles, which says, "I let miracles replace all grievances." I used this guy I hated for years as the object of my forgiveness. It seemed impossible at first; but I stayed with it and did the lesson as was directed in the book...

"Today we go beyond the grievances, to look upon the miracle instead. We will reverse the way you see by not allowing sight to stop before it sees. We will not wait before the shield of hate, but lay it down and gently lift our eyes in silence to behold the Son of God."

"The body's eyes are closed, and as you think of him who grieved you, let your mind be shown the light in him beyond your grievances."

To my amazement, I felt a calm light fill the room, and a peace so deep cover my heart. I saw my friend released from her pain and I saw the young man asking her for forgiveness. I knew she had already forgiven him. This was now my time for forgiveness.

For me, so many years later, I finally had released my burden of resentment as well. To my surprise, forgiving was easy once I forgave myself. I am so grateful this hidden guilt has finally left me and I have found peace.

Who do you want to punish?

They hurt you and you want revenge! You cry out for justice. There's nothing wrong with that is there? So you begin to set in your mind the most convenient, Machiavellian way of retaliation, the perfect lesson that the perpetrator deserves so you can finally be at peace.

Then you realize you need more reasons to justify your vengeance; for perhaps, the original rationale is not now sufficient. If you look for more reasons they will arrive, because you need them in order to fully validate your attack. The moment you have been waiting so anxiously for has finally arrived.

You exacted your revenge; but that's when you realize it did not give you the happiness you were looking for. To the contrary, it throws you into the depths of hell. Perhaps that was what you were seeking. You did not want peace, nor did you want to be happy. Perhaps you only wanted to punish yourself.

Every time you are looking for an additional reason to justify your attacks, you are injecting into your veins the daily dose of pain you need to maintain your self-identity. You play the role of victim, and thus you think you are alive. When the dose no longer gives you the pleasure it gave you, you increase it many more times.

When you attack you think you are lashing out against someone else, but in fact you are attacking yourself. The more violently you do it, the more violently you lash out at yourself, because it is impossible to hurt someone else without hurting ourselves.

If you really wanted peace you would have it. If you really wanted peace, you would forgive. A forgiveness without arrogance, a forgiveness that will bring about peace of mind. Being able to remember without pain is a sign that we are going in the right direction. Ultimately, we are only forgiving ourselves.

You make what you defend against, and by your own defense against it is it real and inescapable. Lay down your arms, and only then do you perceive it false. (ACIM)

Clear your list

When a year begins it is a good time to look at how we felt about the previous one. We can go through our list of resentments and feelings of guilt and take note if we have released them, or have begun to reinforce them with new grievances that we want to keep.

How difficult it sometimes is to take responsibility and recognize that we always choose the feelings we experience. We convince ourselves we have enough reasons to justify the old and new entries to our grievance list; but in reality all these are futile justifications, because resentments and guilt are useless and unwanted in the end.

Does it bring you peace to remember the person that was unfaithful to you, thinking about all the people that wronged you, or to keep imagining ways to tell them what you never dared say before? Perhaps you are making up strategies to get even with them. After spending some time reviewing those scenes in your mind, I assure you that instead of peace you will feel very tired and frustrated. If you continue doing it every day this behavior will become a habit and bitterness will be present in your heart. Your face, your life and everything around you will reflect what you harbor in your heart. Is that really what you want? If not, perhaps it is time to accept that the constant reminder of your past devastation will never bring about the serenity that lives only in the present moment.

Choose again, and stop carrying the burden of the bittersweet and mediocre life you once lived. By thinking differently you will see something different. Understand that by simply dropping the sword you wield against yourself and surrendering to your creative source, you will find rest and guidance in your life. In this idea lies all the help you need, and this will be manifest in a way you least expect.

Clear your list because it is the only way to regain peace in your soul. Your tool for doing so is forgiveness. Now is the best time to start.

Attacking myself

Stories of forgiveness: Marcela
Her testimony

My story began 35 years ago with what I call the event that ended my childhood. At that time, my father had had an affair with another woman. As a result of that relationship he had three more children. The woman had kept the children away from my father and he started to sink into gambling, alcoholism and a deep depression. My mother meanwhile, began to develop a deep rage and resentment in her heart which was expressed with physical and psychological abuse towards my brothers and me.

One day when I was 12 years old, my mother had gone out and locked the room that had access to the only TV in the house. Completely bored, I remembered how film characters opened such padlocks with a small wire. So I said to myself, "I can do that." I searched among the shelves and found a wooden stick which I thought might work. Of course it immediately broke inside the lock and a great fear came over me. I knew my mother's wrath could be immense and it terrified me to think what she might do.

When she arrived I started to shake and sweat. I had a feeling something was going to happen. I watched, petrified, as she put her key in the lock and it got stuck. I could have stayed silent. I could have pretended to have nothing to do with it, but then, a deep sense of responsibility for what happened made me speak.

"I did it", I said. "I broke the lock because I wanted to watch TV."

Immediately all her anger and frustration turned on me. I first felt a blow on my back, and then I watched, as she returned, enraged, and tried to open the door again. Unable to get it, she rammed her body against me many times, hitting me on my arms, legs and back. I remember screaming for help, crying, and trying to resist the extent of her violence. In a show of survival, I escaped into the only place I knew I could lock the door from the inside, the bathroom. At that moment her anger grew and she began to beat on the door with her feet and hands. I resisted, crying and calling out for help as much as I could. After a few minutes, I felt the door was being battered so I decided to open it. Again, I thought it was my duty, as the house in which we lived was rented and I knew at that time we did not have the means to pay for a new door. I knew the moment that I removed the lock from the door I would face her insane anger. I wouldn't resist. I totally surrendered to her rage and could only ask God for help.

Voluntarily, I unlocked the door that kept me safe. My tears were running down my face. Immediately I was pulled heavily by one of my arms. I struggled to keep from falling to the floor. To my surprise, every one of her blows did not hurt as much as the hatred expressed in them.

When she was tired of beating me, my older sister appeared with the padlock in her hands, completely fixed. A neighbor who had heard my cries came to ask what was happening. He took the lock and removed the piece of wood that obstructed it. All of the sudden, all my mom's anger ceased. I could feel the amazement and relief when she realized that the door was in place and fully functioning. For me it had the opposite effect. The young girl I once was died that day, and in her place was a bitter woman of 12 years old.

From that moment on it was impossible to allow a caress from my mother. The touch of her hand trying to fix my hair or an attempted hug was quite uncomfortable. Ever since that moment, our communication was broken. I grew up avoiding both physical and emotional contact as well. I was never able to tell her what it was in my heart, my successes, my failures, my heartache in the times when my heart was broken. Everything was hidden from her, because I locked my emotions in a mental prison in which I felt safe. From that moment, I refused any expression of love that came from her hand. I considered it false, because for me, nothing would justify such extraordinary violence against someone you love.

When I saw other mothers embracing their daughters of my age, I was quite surprised and thought, "How can they allow themselves to be embraced."

Many years later when I began my spiritual journey,

I realized that she did not hate me. I felt how much we had suffered together for my rejection of her over the years. The hatred of her punches was not directed towards me but towards herself. It was the hatred of her own miserable drama of her own existence. Discovering this made me see her with compassion, and recognize that all my life I had relived that moment of terror as a means of self-aggression.

I never wanted to accept her forgiveness because I wanted to use that pain to continue hurting myself. She was not the attacker anymore. It was me, attacking myself with my own thoughts.

When I relinquished the suffering, I could free myself and release her at the same time. Forgiveness appeared as a spring of light that healed my mind and spirit.

My heart is free of resentment now and I am very happy to see her, to talk to her and share my spiritual experiences. Her aged face shows me all her love and tenderness which was never absent from her heart. Now I can embrace her and express how much I love her. Little remains of the tough facade of the woman from years ago. I can see God in her and feel a great love within her as well. The past has stopped having effects on my present, and now I can only experience the peace that comes through forgiving love.

Now I can truly say,

"I Love You, Mom."

I seek a future different from the past

A well known definition of insanity is: "Doing the same thing over and over again and expecting a different result." It is a brilliant statement that reflects the condition of the human mind. In fact, if you are reading this sentence and have not yet begun to doubt your senses, then read it again.

The amazing thing is, we not only do the same thing expecting a different result, but we then blame the world for not getting the result we want. We explain everything that has happened to us since the beginning of time with poor reasoning based on our limited perception. We could argue that our condition is due to bad luck, our unjust childhood, the opposite sex, the country where we were born, or just perhaps our karma; but our problems have nothing to do with any of those things. They have to do with that pervasive and paralyzing feeling innate to the human condition, fear.

It is fear that is keeping us from stepping out of our comfort zone, and it is also the reason we repeat our discouraging routines. Even though we feel tired, we don't do anything to change it.

We get up every morning at the set time, have breakfast, go to work, then return, have dinner, rest and when we finally stop to take a breath, we realize we have spent twenty years doing the same thing. Perhaps, we always wanted to share more with our family, travel more, study something else, start the project we've neglecting, learn another language, or simply be free.

We have become accustomed to wandering aimlessly in our mind between a shadowy past and an uncertain future. We suffer and exhaust ourselves, trying to solve problems that do not even exist. We are so terrified to think differently; however, therein lies our salvation.

If we want a future different from the past, we have to start changing our thinking in the present. We must leave behind our stories of self-pity and ask that a new way of seeing the world be shown to us.

We can choose again in every moment. It will never be too late to do this. Trust that everything that seems to happen to us can be used for our rebirth. However, changing our destructive thoughts requires the act of daily mental training, along with our total willingness.

What if, every morning when we wake up, we fill ourselves with a rich and powerful thought to embrace throughout the day? Later on, when we are crushed by despair, or just feel a twinge of anger in our heart, we can use it. Remember that the world we picture will be transformed by changing our thoughts. One such thought will be a lifesaver that we can hold on to whenever we need. It will rescue us from our mental wreckage in a single instant.

Here are some of those life saving thoughts:

I am never upset for the reason I think *
I have given everything I see all the meaning it has for me *
My mind is preoccupied with past thoughts *
Above all I want to see things differently *
God is the strength in which I trust *
There is another way of seeing the world *
Let miracles replace all grievances *
I could see peace instead of this *
and therefore...
There is nothing to fear *

What if you start to feel peace, and open the door to a greater experience of truth and light . Give it a try!

*Lessons from A Course In Miracles.

Remember always that you cannot be anywhere
except in the Mind of God. When you forget
this, you will despair and you will attack. (ACIM)

Who is your enemy?

There are some days when we feel that everyone is against us, every move we make is used by others to hurt us and diminish our self-esteem.

All of the sudden we realize that we have spent much of our lives feeling like the sorrowful target of one person or another. We think that if that individual would not be against us, we would be at peace. However, if the person who was allegedly attacking us ceases to do so, there usually is a new one in his place, and everything starts all over again.

But what can we do, when apparently people insist on making our life impossible? Why everybody agrees in making us feel inadequate? When those who attack us will stop doing so?

Let´s think about it. Would it be possible that all the people that surround us could agree on the same thing? Could it be possible that we have found ourselves surrounded by chaos because we have accepted it as a normal part of life? What about taking on a new perspective, a way to see things differently?

What if, in the habit of taking everything personally, the perceived attacks were only magnified by the lens of our perception?

Maybe the server in the restaurant, who did not attend us as we wanted, was concerned about the health of his child, or the coworker that frowned at us did not even notice us in his line of sight.

Maybe that person you thought was talking about you was really saying something nice.

Most of what we call adversity is the result of the projection of our ideas, and all of them can change. It is just a temporary condition. It is not an unchangeable state.

The only thing that has to change is my mind. It is just me. When I surrender, there is no one left to fight, except myself. The revenge I want only inflicts pain on myself, because actually, my enemy was me.

Wrong Again

Stories of forgiveness: Laura
Her testimony

For some time I had been planning a Christmas greeting for my family. I had been living in Europe with my boyfriend for a couple of years and wanted to give them a warm greeting in a non-traditional way. After much thought, I had the idea to write a little reflection on the true meaning of Christmas and share a passage from A Course in Miracles. After saying each of their names in turn, my message ended with, "I love you." So, on Christmas Eve, I called my family and read them my reflection letter over the phone. A few seconds after finishing my reading, I heard the old, familiar, sarcastic comments from my father towards my mother, regarding parts of my message. Then came her immediate defensive reaction, and then his counter reaction. He, being drunk, became very aggressive, adding some derogatory remarks.

Thus began a conflict between the two. That was the

moment I decided to hang up. I could not process what I was hearing. I just observed how a beautiful melody could suddenly be transformed into a dissonant noise.

The following week, I spoke with my mother, who, still trapped in the anger towards my father, kept complaining about his attitude toward her. However, she made no allusion of appreciation for the Christmas message I sent to them. There I was, with no desire of believing what I was hearing, faced with this absurd scenario, experiencing of all the resistance that human beings seem to have in receiving love. They had superimposed the ego over a manifestation of affection. I spent some time thinking and wondering in my mind about this feeling of total frustration in my relationship with my parents. I could not believe my open message of love had been the catalyst for a family conflict. Something must be very wrong with this family, and I of course, was included.

I began to remember my inability to accept my mother's life had always revolved around the views of my father. His opinions were of so much value to her that her total mood, even her health, were always affected by them. Since their relationship was always bad, her life was always unhappy and full of disease. I could not understand how she could not get the message of love expressed in my phone call? or even enjoy the "I Love You" I sincerely meant for her. What did it matter if he mocked her? His opinion did not change who she was. That was my message to her, but she had not accepted it.

I tortured myself with these thoughts for a few days, until I discovered, what I was doing with my mom was exactly what she had done with my dad. Just before I reached total disappointment, I remembered one sentence from my spiritual studies, "My only function is to give love no matter what the outcome." At that moment, I realized the futility of continually circling around what I considered good or bad, fair or unfair. Just for a moment I allowed myself to be wrong, for I remembered, ultimately we are always wrong.

We all depend on insane thoughts of external approval to function in this world. In my case it was my mother and my father. For others it may be their boss, their kids or their social network. Even to me at that time, I expected to receive the thanks of my family. When I did not receive it, I had the perfect excuse to keep my grievances. Maybe that was what I wanted, an excuse to hold onto my resentments.

To restore my peace of mind I had to drop my judgments completely. Not just a few, but all of them. Now, without them, I found myself watching the irrational race undertaken by all humans in search of love, irrational because we seek it where it cannot be found, outside ourselves. What we are looking for is within. Every action is said to be either love or a call for help, and that is how we need to look at it. All the aggressiveness of my family was no more than a call for help. It was not an attack against me. Now all I can do is offer all my love to them.

"Understand that you do not respond to anything directly, but to your interpretation of it. Your interpretation thus becomes the justification for the response. That is why analyzing the motives of others is hazardous to you. If you

decide that someone is really trying to attack you or desert you or enslave you, you will respond as if he had actually done so, having made his error real to you. To interpret error is to give it power, and having done this you will overlook truth."
ACIM.

When you are sad, know this need not be.
Depression comes from a sense of being
deprived of something you want and do not
have. Remember that you are deprived of
nothing except by your own decisions, and then
decide otherwise. (ACIM)

What remains when everything is over?

I have experienced death in many ways in my life, and I have realized that I don´t need to be to be six feet underground in order to be in hell. I die whenever anger, depression or a sense of hopelessness takes me over.

We have all pursued our happiness in a world where we long to have money, properties, recognition, sex, a life partner; however, once we possess all of this, we realize that it is not enough. We still feel incomplete and sad because everything we see in this world is uncertain, temporary and ephemeral.

We were sure we would find eternal happiness in earthly things. Holding these things before us we chased after them, crawling up from the bottom our devastation, trying to catch the last little crumbs of satisfaction from the world. We leaned eagerly toward the abyss in an awkward final attempt to find happiness.

We begin an anxious race to death in a cycle that has repeated itself again and again in this pantomime of pain and suffering that we call life.

And once again we are in the abyss. Once again, we are in darkness.

We were looking for eternal happiness in something that was not eternal. We were seeking for it in the midst of mirages and got lost there.

When everything ends we realize that the only thing left is God. When we surrender and put down our weapons we will be able to realize we have always had everything we needed. It was just in the only place we had not searched, inside of us. When we quiet the noise of our mind we can finally hear the wisdom of the voice that speaks for God. What seemed confused and chaotic gets washed clean, and we understand if we let Him lead the way everything will serve a greater purpose than we could ever imagine.

Listen as his gentle voice constantly reminds you, "There is nothing to fear, I will never forsake you."

When everything is over is a time for celebration. It means we have reached a point where we can make a radical change in our life. We can spring from there and turn it into total dependence on God. It is no longer worth it to pursue the truth with limited potentials when we have all the power of the universe within us.

If we allow forgiveness and love to be the focus of our life we will reach heaven in this very moment.

Welcome change!

Expect a Miracle

Have you ever wondered why, when all is well, things seem to be going smoothly in our world and we are apparently happy, the joy quickly fades? Have you ever thought that happiness is only the prelude to some adversity, as if a scathing destiny played with us, giving us a few instants of pleasure only to show us the face of death a moment later?

If this has happened to you, it is not because there is a cosmic ruse against the happy people; but because at some point you expected it to be so.

We are very attentive to the arrival of conflict, and actually want it to arrive so the ego can say with pride, "I knew it." It is the reason the jealous insist on finding hard facts that can destroy their relationship, when meanwhile, they spend hours mesmerizing themselves with the thought of the moment when they discover the betrayal. It is the reason we make ourselves ill by holding on to past grievances and also the reason why we build turmoil around us. In our fear we expect a loved one to die, an accident, a robbery, something to happen to our children, to be fired from a job, an incurable disease or financial disaster. We live our life in a permanent state of fear, breathing it into the world around us each day. What we are expecting is death itself

All of this is simply happening in our mind. All these frightening ideas are solely a product of our wrong thinking. Why are we waiting for hell? Why not expect a miracle instead?

Just for an instant, look at the thoughts that rush into your mind every time you enter into a moment of silence. Look at how many of the ideas that come to you are disturbing. Where are they? They live only in your mind and you give them the power to become your reality.

Be still and see an idea to which you are very afraid. Choose the most devastating scenario of which you can conceive. You may occasionally have been assaulted by that thought in the middle of the night, waking up with your heart beating out of your chest. Perhaps this fear remains dormant in your mind like a beast waiting to attack at the slightest slip.

When you know clearly what is your greatest fear, tell yourself, "this does not have to be." Then ask yourself, "what do I get out of this situation? Why do I want this situation, if it will make me unhappy?" The answer should reach you loud and clear. I would rather be wrong and be happy. If I do not get anything positive from this I do not want it. Satisfying my ego never offers tranquility. Each time that another thought of fear comes to your mind say to yourself: "That tragedy is of no use to me. This disease is of no use to me. Insanity is of no use to me."

The natural state of your life is not suffering. Miracles are your natural state and you are entitled to them. Start today to reverse each thought that does not bring you peace, because those thoughts are not natural.

From this time forward, open your mind to experience true happiness. It is a constant exercise in which you start changing the craziness of your ideas by using thoughts that bring you peace. You are not asked to not have any ideas of fear, but to not have any that you would keep. Begin your practice today. If you do it every day you will gain certainty that what is natural for you is the fullness and joy of life. Soon this idea will become consistent in your mind as a constant reminder.

If you change your thoughts, you change your reality. You can do whatever you want, here and now. There is no other time. You cannot do it in the past or in the future. Why wait for the worst? Expect a miracle instead.

Addiction to pain

An addiction could be defined as the uncontrolled engagement in obsessive behavior by an individual. This refers not only to the consumption of substances such as alcohol, drugs, food or cigarettes; but also to the so-called non-toxic addictions, including one that might seem strange yet familiar to us, addiction to pain.

Examine your life and see if there are patterns that repeat over and over again. Do you find yourself jumping from one conflict to another with different characters? Are you reliving the same situation everywhere you seem to go, no matter who you seem to be with? Such was case with the woman whose father, husband and son were all alcoholics; the person who was repeatedly abused, betrayed and abandoned by her partners, the man who feels humiliated in every one of his jobs, families who have experienced the same diseases for generations, or the people who experience periodic situations of financial deprivation or perhaps are taken by shady business practices.

Do you think that these patterns are coincidental? Have you ever considered the possibility of having an internal saboteur who makes you addicted to pain?

You may not like to hear this, but the saboteur is you. Without being aware of it, you feel attracted to situations that will ultimately end up hurting you. It is as if a part of you begins to recognize you are entering into voluntary failure, but, paradoxically, that is what most appeals to you. Your insane mind constantly seeks this frustration and that is why it is your mind that needs healing.

The first step, as with any addiction, is to recognize that you need help.

Try to identify every situation that you have created to accentuate your status of victim or perpetrator. Find the patterns you have repeated. Search your mind. Surely you will find something you have overlooked. What is behind your inclination towards abusive relationships, or your continued financial failure? There is an underlying idea behind these patterns, and you can find it.

Maybe compiling a list would be helpful. Choose a time when you can be completely alone and start writing. For example: describe in one word how your last relationship ended. You might be surprised. Note if more than once the terms such as abandonment or infidelity are repeated. You can do the same by writing the reason you had to change your old job, or what bothers you about you current one. Is it your boss, your co-workers, your salary? Once you have identified the pattern, such as abandonment in your relationships, stop right there. Identify it and recognize it is very important.

Do not reject it nor take lightly. If abandonment is what you have continually seen in your life, it is because you have been attracted to it. I know this is a pretty radical idea, but at the same time, the one which will allow for your healing.

The second step is to take responsibility. The universe is not against you. The particular situation that overwhelms you will continue to present itself, until it no longer has any value to you.

If you have taken responsibility for your own pain, you have probably already noticed that there was something that attracted you to it. You valued it because, unconsciously, you felt guilty and craved punishment. Healing will come to reverse that thought system. If you forgive and accept your innocence you will no longer have any need to be punished.

If you now wonder why you would have to consider yourself innocent, the answer is simpler than you think. It is because no one has condemned you. God wants you to stop condemning yourself, because His only desire for you is perfect happiness.

The third step is to accept that the will of God for me is perfect happiness.

When you replace blame with forgiveness, a veil is lifted before your eyes. You will look with love on the ones you used to hate and thus, you start to love again. If you forgive yourself, you will realize that your inheritance is happiness, not pain.

We are not victims of the world we see and we are not guilty. We have made mistakes because we have listened the voice of the ego instead of the voice of our inner wisdom. What we are apparently living in is a dream of suffering, from which we can awaken any time we choose.

Make a decision from the depths of your being and break the pattern of self-abuse that you have been living in. Reject the thoughts that will not bring you peace and let them go. If a false thought comes into your mind, repeat, *"I will forgive and this will disappear"* (Lesson 193 ACIM).

Ask for help and see that it always comes immediately. Stay in the Now. You are not alone. You have never been alone.

God's Will is perfect happiness for me. And I can suffer but from the belief there is another will apart from His. (ACIM)

Why are you here?

Do you know how vast our universe is? Do you have any idea how much time has passed since its origin? Perhaps you're not interested in these subjects. But why, you may ask, do we wonder about the stars, if we need to be here anchored to the world, worrying about paying the rent, the education of our children, car payments, being in fashion, or other "relevant" matters. What do we care if there is something beyond our vision, if finally, in the midst of the darkened days of our cities fouled air we will not even be able to look up see the sky.

Let's take a look at how satisfying our lives are right now. We wake up every day, at the same time, we eat the same breakfast, go to work, do the same job for eight to twelve hours, come home tired, repeat the routine the next day and receive money in return. However, in some place in our mind, a bittersweet, frustration appears. We know we can do much better; but despite that feeling, we keep repeating our days as if we didn't have another option. We have followed the requirements of the world, have a career, marriage, job, car, house and children. We should be happy, but we are not.

Sometimes we try to spice up the routine by adding some excitement to our lives. We perhaps sedate ourselves with alcohol, drugs and dysfunctional relationships, without noticing that we are getting engaged in activities that will bring even more unhappiness to us.

Deep in your heart, you are longing for something more than what the world can offer you. What you want is not in alignment with a self-imposed routine. There is a part of yourself who dares to question your current role in your life and to seek for help. Listen to it!

Our purpose is something that we cannot grasp with a limited consciousness, something that is not materialized in the temporal world. This purpose can only be clear for us when we listen to the voice of love within us, when we stop hating and free ourselves from our resentments, when we feel a part of God and live like it. Then everything will make sense, then we will understand that the only thing that will give meaning to our life is love, and that its inevitable consequence is perfect happiness.

You are here to provide a light to the world, and extend the healing of your mind; to bear witness to the infinite power of love and the healing power of forgiveness. That is your true function. That is why you are here.

Why is it difficult to forgive?

It seems hard to forgive because we think that there is someone outside our self attacking us but, in truth, we are only attacking ourselves.

We are unable to forgive because it means losing the self-identity that we have been working to perfect. We may have built this identity as a victim of a wife's betrayal, as the employee that everyone abuses at work, as a mother of a drug-addicted child, or a person who was abused by his parents. All these labels are part of your identity. To forgive would mean losing the excuse you are using to justify your suffering.

We are holding on to resentments that somehow have become very "comfortable" for us. Just look at how a woman could introduce herself from this perspective:

"Nice to meet you, I am Mary Adams, four times betrayed by my husband and mother of one alcoholic son."

But, if she let that identity go, how would she introduce herself to the world now, as a happy person?

81

That would be unthinkable because she is proud of the victim status that she has forged.

Now, let us focus on you.

Bring to your mind that "unforgivable" act that was done to you. Very likely you will begin to feel an increase in your internal energy and that will translate into heat and adrenaline. Feel it! Remember that villain that hurt you! The one who stole something from you, humiliated you, betrayed you and made you feel like a victim. You are at the mercy of a cruel world. Now, look at the prison, where you have placed the one who caused you such pain. Look at yourself! You are chained to the one you won't forgive.

For a long time he, or she, has been your most beloved partner. You have brought them with you everywhere you went. He or she has been in your most special moments, tormenting you. And you are still faithful to your tormentor, reliving the moment of pain again and again! Now, look closely. Who is hurting you? Is it the perpetrator? No! You are doing it to yourself!

You think you won't be able to forgive because their pain would be released and, "they don't deserve it" but actually, you don't forgive them because you think you will be released from the pain, and you do not deserve it ... but you do deserve it!

You are chained to your past and to your pain. Look into your heart and find the key to the prison door. If you open that door and let them out, you will also be free.

What bothers me about others?

Once, while working on a new project at my old company, we were suddenly informed that Daniela would be our new boss. Some of us had previously worked with her and knew well of her authoritarian attitude. On the other hand, we also learned that another colleague, Magda, would join the team shortly. Joseph and I looked at each other without saying a word, we knew that this combination would be explosive. The two did not know each other, but they were very much alike.

Of course, it was not long after we started working in the same office with Daniela, when she began to have conflicts with Magda. Both complained about similar things. Each one resented the behavior of the other, but neither one realized they were acting in the same way. There was no way they understood what bothered them about the other. What actually bothered them of course, was something within themselves.

Since both had found themselves doing a job they hated, they saw in each other the reflection of their own frustration. My friend, Joseph, and I watched everything in silence without interfering or encouraging any of their mutual complaints. In a short time each one decided to go to work at a different job.

It was very easy for Joseph and I to understand why neither of them could stand each other, but impossible for the two coworkers to realize this. A shiver ran down my spine when I thought of some people who I did not like. Those with whom I had never had much patience, those who I had hated at times and the ones I had judged as well. Would they also be showing me aspects of myself that I did not like?

I tried to resist this idea, as if trying to hold off an avalanche using only my bare hands. Had I behaved like those people who had irritated me so much?

Never!

Impossible!

But then I recognized myself in Daniela, complaining about Magda. All of a sudden time stopped around me. I saw myself standing in her shoes, wearing her clothes, doing exactly the same thing. I did not realize my own behavior.

I had endlessly criticized the attitude of those who bothered me and had never noticed it was my own. However, if I wanted healing I had to be fair; if I wanted to be fair, I had to include everyone. I couldn't make any exceptions, especially with the ones I had more resistance with. They were the ones who would show me what needed to be healed in me.

I slowly laid down my defenses. In each case, I recognized with amazement, my own behavior. Once I stopped resisting, I began to see my own reflection in each of the people who had passed through my life. Now I could see my reactions objectively from above the battlefield. I could now accept that many of the reactions I had to others were merely a reflection of my own judgments.

From that moment on, I started to observe what was happening in my mind when I did not like someone. If I was tempted to start pouring out my judgments and complaints, I stopped and asked for help to see what was really bothering me. The answer always came by showing me something related to how I was feeling about myself.

All of this experience taught me that if we want peace of mind, healing is inevitable, although it may come in the most unexpected ways.

Take a moment to look around. What you see is a reflection of your thoughts. Focus on those who disturb you. Can you see parts of yourself in them? You will discover much more than you think and ultimately you will be able to forgive what bothers you about yourself.

Later on, I found Daniela smiling and happy. After quitting her job she had started a new career as a therapist. Magda, meanwhile, became a speaker. Once they started doing what they loved, they welcomed joy into their lives. When you find healing in your mind someone else will find it too. It is impossible to be healed alone.

"When I am healed I'm not healed alone. And I would bless my brothers, for I would be healed with them, as they are healed with me." ACIM

I will not value what is valueless, and only what has value do I seek, for only that do I desire to find. (ACIM)

New year's gift

Stories of forgiveness: Jennifer
Her testimony

Due to the huge amount of mail sent late on December 30, my friend, Julia, and I received an emergency call to assist in the mail room, shipping packages. All the packages had to be distributed from our little town to different offices of our company in the U.S. Our shift manager, Ronald, announced that we would work with Clare, who was responsible for that section.

After a few minutes, we saw our colleague entering the office, who aggressively rushed to open the curtains. Full of anger and with a huge air of arrogance, she asked our names and then proceeded to start working.

We proceeded to do our work using common sense because we did not receive any directions from Clare. We did the work the way we thought was most logical. Clare realized this and started yelling and grumbling, mocking the procedures we used. In her mind she perceived that we were not doing things the way she felt was right. She was continuously screaming at us for her work tools, even though we didn't know they belonged to her. When we finished organizing the customer mail, she would return to re-classify it to her liking. The whole scene became incoherent, almost like a strange satire. Nevertheless, thanks to her attitude and behavior, I could clearly see how we create our own conflicts.

We do not communicate with those around us, and yet, we hope that others act the way we think they should. When they do not, we get frustrated, feeding our anger and sense of injustice. We are not aware of our responsibility in creating the chaos we see.

For Julia and me it was absolutely clear that Clare kept a huge grudge in her heart, and although her attacks on us were very direct and recurrent, at no time did we take them personally. For we both knew that this day could become a complete hell, if we let ourselves react in the same way she did, giving her resentments power to dictate her actions.

In a quiet moment, I closed my eyes and lifted my spirit, asking for help and the wisdom to act. The next instant, she asked if I had locked the door to the other office where we had been working earlier. I told her, "I did not". Her face began to transfigure with anger before my eyes. So, I said with calm certainty, "Just tell me if you want me to do it and I will be happy to." To which, she then agreed, and I eagerly went and locked the door. Upon returning, I saw with surprise how kindly she began to explain to me and Julia all the procedures of the work. Gradually, to our astonishment, the angry lady was completely transformed.

Upon reaching the third office, we encountered a totally different person. In a friendly manner, Clare offered and served us coffee. Although a latent frustration remained in her tone, she began to tell us a little of her story.

Her husband was an alcoholic and a drug addict; she hated her job, but had to wait another year to return to her own country. In the midst of her desperation, I saw her eyes filled with tears. At that point I said, "But you know that you can change your life." She looked at me with hope in her face and replied, "Yes, but I need one more year to go back home and meet with my son."

After a few hours work, Ronald, our manager, suggested that one of us should go to another section. With her gaze alone, my old "enemy" motioned for me to stay with her. As we continued working, she asked me about my family, to which I replied, "They were all well and my husband was a wonderful man."

She did not stop thanking me every time we finished a portion of our work. We were moving with amazing speed with ease and flow. She told me she spoke five languages: Russian, Polish, Ukrainian, French and English. We shared some phrases in those languages and ended up singing a Christmas song together.

After a while, my friend, Julia, returned to join us. Clare was doubly grateful because she had also done an excellent job.

We ended half an hour ahead of schedule, at which point Claire received a phone call, and I overheard her saying, "I'm working with two beautiful girls." Every time we needed her tools, she lent them to us in a very pleasant and helpful manner.

At the end of the day, she said she was very pleased to meet us. And then, in a very sweet tone, she added "Happy New Year!

Author's Note

I propose an experiment: when you are at your workplace, in your office or with your family, and feel that someone is attacking you, do not rush to answer. Do not take attitudes personally and remember we are never upset for the reason we think. Instead of reacting the same way, take a few seconds and ask for inspiration to act wisely. An action of your mind can completely change the panorama of your life. The moment you drop your defenses and stop trying to arrange things your way, the miracle appears.

Allow the One who knows to guide you.

You might be surprised.

You may experience a miracle.

Illness: what is it for?

Until recently, I thought that diseases occurred because they were natural. Perhaps they could even be the result of some mystical punishment, or occur for a number of different reasons. However, I had never entertained the idea that illnesses were more prone to arise in our moments of despair.

At one point in my life, I began to realize that depressed people got sick more often than happy people. After experiencing periods of trauma, individuals can also develop certain types of physical conditions, or become more accident prone. Something was connected in a way that I did not, as yet, understand. These occurrences could not be mere coincidence, but had to somehow be related to the thought process in the minds of the afflicted.

Without really intending to, I started paying attention to the people around me who seemed to get ill. Diana, for example, began to suffer from a rare eye condition that affected her from the moment her ex-husband began to seek custody of her youngest daughter. Once the case was resolved in her favor, she was healed of her condition. Federico, a family friend, began to suffer from severe pain in his lower back after he was fired from his job. Once he began to follow his true passion, his back was also healed. And there was Mariana, who began to experience an unusual allergic condition in her legs at the same time she learned that she and her husband were in bankruptcy.

In all these cases, the disease materialized in the aftermath of a substantial traumatic event in their lives. In each case, their physical ailments increased as their concerns grew.

This need not be. Every challenge we go through is an opportunity of growth, just by changing the perspective of the situation we find a smoother way to overcome a circumstance. When we change our minds everything around us changes as well.

Anger and fear leave our bodies vulnerable; but these emotions first arise in our thoughts and then accumulate in the body. The cure, therefore, must be directed toward healing of the mind. We cannot try to cure the body without healing the source of the condition. If we try to do so we would only be providing a superficial cure, and under similar circumstances the condition may immediately manifest in the body once again. Instead, the healed mind recognizes it has no use for disease and won't use the body as an instrument of punishment. It uses it instead as a witness to the freedom and wholeness of the individual.

Fear vanishes when we are confident that we have not been abandoned, nor do we have to rely on our own strength. When we recognize we can use the divine strength of God within, then we can use it wisely and peace can return to our minds.

Anger, on the other hand, is generated by lack of forgiveness. It is a poison we drink voluntarily. It is the fuel of all resentments. When we welcome forgiveness, we see our anger disappear. A stream of light envelopes our being, cleansing all our wounds so we can continue on our journey with joy and serenity.

We will replace our tears of sorrow with happiness and gratitude.

Healing is a decision we can make. To heal we must be aware of the fact that there is no value in disease, and therefore, we do not need it. Do not give value to what has none. Our work has just begun. It is time to trust and forgive. Wholeness is our natural state.

So poignantly He calls to you that you will not resist Him longer. In that instant He will take you to His home, and you will stay with Him in perfect stillness, silent and at peace, beyond all words, untouched by fear and doubt, sublimely certain that you are at home.(ACIM)

A Great Discovery

After having a conversation with a close friend, it became clear in my consciousness the ease with which humans can cherish a grievance. We allow, justify and defend so much, we make it the focus of our existence.

With great frustration, my friend, Marcia, described how much she had been unhappy with her children and her husband for many years. This was nothing new. What would be a novelty was what was about to be revealed to me. As our conversation progressed, and she continued complaining about her family, I noticed her special ability to reverse any situation and make it a resounding attack upon herself. All these attacks were only in her imagination. As a close friend of hers, I witnessed the respect and love, especially her children professed for her. However, Marcia had built an impenetrable shell against every sign of affection that her close relatives would attempt show her.

As soon as I hung up the phone, I tried to clear my thoughts. For a few seconds, I wanted to mentally review the conversation we had. However, I gave up almost immediately because I saw the futility of wanting to understand the insanity of human behavior. The idea that haunted my mind was that it would be very easy to be finished with all the pain we experience, if only we could see that we are the cause of our own misery. If we could use a different perception other than the one we have been using to hurt ourselves, hate would disappear. However, to do so we would have to start thinking differently. We would have to open a window in our constrained mind to behold the freedom, the bliss, and the peace to which we would have access if we truly desired.

So I decided to apply those ideas for myself and made a decision not to judge Marcia. Then something very interesting happened. I saw myself having the same feelings as Marcia. It seemed as if now I were in her skin, as if I were her, experiencing the same feelings she was. Then I remembered how, some years before, I had gone through a painful breakup. At that point, I thought about something interesting. I considered that my partner's love had never been sincere. It was much less painful to consider this than to think, at one time it had been genuine, but somehow changed. I realized that I had behaved exactly like Marcia. I had chosen the roll of victim. I rejected the possibility that I had been loved, and at the same time, started to go deep in destructive thoughts against myself.

Those destructive thoughts were a false sense of strength. I had enclosed myself in a sealed box where I thought I was safe in order to ease my pain, or at least that's what I believed at the time.

Recognizing I had behaved the same way as Marcia made me want to understand my own reasoning. I then realized, if I understood myself, I would understand her too. If I let myself be healed, I would not be healed alone. She would be healed as well. My question now was, why did I want to lock myself in the same kind of armored fortress, and more importantly, why had this apparently eased my pain?

The response was more amazing than I had ever imagined. It was a revelation that opened my eyes. If I convinced myself that I had never been loved, I would be justified in keeping my resentments. If I had a consistent justification for them, I could live my life without the need to forgive, and finally, if I had accepted I was loved, I would have to love also, and I did not want to.

So that was the whole story, mine, Marcia's, and all the people who remain resentful and disgusted by their past. Denial of forgiveness is the same as the negation of love. If we forgive, we have to love. But is that what we want?

If we forgive, we have to drop our resentments, but sometimes we are so attached to them, like a hardened crust in our souls. Our resentments make us cringe, make us sick, steal our peace of mind, yet we value them so much that we cannot imagine our life without them. We think we would die if we were to get rid of them. In fact, the only thing that could happen is the opposite. We would actually begin to live for the first time.

When we choose to forgive we come out of the

darkness, we see such a bright and peaceful universe. We will never want to return to the darkness of our judgments. We can experience an absolute love for those we once hated. We can start to see God in each of his creations, and feeling a part of them, we see God in ourselves.

The release is in your hands. Welcome to Life and to Light. You have spent a lot of time wandering helplessly. Open your mind and your arms to receive the infinite love that is ready for you.

Remember this always: *Forgiveness is the key to happiness.*

I rest in God today, and let Him work in me and through me, while I rest in Him in quiet and in perfect certainty. (ACIM)

You are not a body, you are free.

In memory of Mauricio

When a loved one goes away the intense pain we experience can destroy the world we have built around us. At times we seem to have no reason to live. We have based our entire well-being on world that seemed solid, without realizing how fragile and perishable it was. Now, despite the advice from friends and their good intentions to help us to come out of our agony, our strength is exhausted. We think we will never be able to wake up from the nightmare.

What is it that really makes you hurt? Is it guilt? Is it what you never told them when you had the chance? Is it perhaps, just the absence of the body, the emptiness of the physical space that your loved one seemed to occupy? Do you look to that space framed by carbon, hydrogen and oxygen to find the one you loved? Do you look there to see that figure that seemed so solid, the one you seemed to touch and you seemed to love. For a moment you thought your loved one was just a body

100

and that is not true.

Can you feel on some level of your being that you and those around you are much more than a simple physical configuration? The love you feel for your loved ones can keep you in touch with them, even if they are no longer visible to you. Love goes far beyond the barriers of matter. If we had a glimpse of what this means, all sorrow and sense of loss would fade. We are spirit, and we are always connected to each other. Our true self surpasses our human perceptions, and on that level, we remain in constant communication where no words are needed.

How would you feel if you lived in the certainty that those who left this continuum of time abide in an unbreakable connection with you and with everything? Those who left this place are on a different plane of consciousness and you have no arguments to prove they are not in perfect peace.

Would you still be anchored to pain if you knew what we call life is indeed a nightmare, a dream of death from which we can wake up? What logic is there to come to a tiny planet in an infinite universe, exist there a few years and gradually experience the loss of all we love, which seems to tear us apart when it happens? Would we not have a more important goal than to merely survive and wait for death? Do you really think that an absolutely perfect, kind and loving creator sent you to this world to suffer, and He is also responsible for your loss?

There is a different way of seeing the world. There is a reality that is not visible to the eyes of the body, a reality that can only come as an experience. This will show you that you are perfectly supported and can continually enjoy the peace of God. It is available to you the moment you decide that the miracle is part of you.

The Miracle is you!

You have all the help you need.

Start by saying to yourself:

I am not a body, I am free, for I am still as God created me.

(Lesson 199 A Course in Miracles.)

Who is judging you?

It is a common habit for us as human beings to observe everything that happens around us and give it a qualification. But judging is more than a bad habit. It is an addiction that puts us on an imaginary throne from which we are able to monitor everyone and bestow value judgments about everything they do. By doing this we feel a malicious pleasure, and the more we question others, the more our ego feeds like a leech. The satisfaction that comes from judgment is a sorrowful satisfaction. Soon enough we begin to feel more miserable than those we were judging. We were criticizing in others what we could not stand in ourselves.

During an experiment held by an important shoe company, participants were asked to rate each of their colleagues with an adjective that, in their opinion, best defined each employee. The options for adjectives were: productive, inefficient, or obsessive. At the end of the session each participant realized he was graded mostly with the same adjective that he had assigned to his peers. If a participant rated his peers on average as inefficient eighty percent of the time, he/she also was rated as inefficient by his/her colleagues. The same happened with the adjectives "productive" and "obsessive." Whatever evaluation was given out had a high probability of being the same received. This example shows that what we see in others is a reflection of what we are projecting ourselves.

Pay attention to the way your mind works. Watch your thoughts and notice the moment you start to make a judgment. How useful is this judgment? Does it bring you peace? And above all, what about yourself do you see in the one you are criticizing? Think about it. Watch your mind. Stay there for a moment, in silence. Try to let go the avalanche of thoughts that come to you every second. If these are not easily released, watch them, without judging them and then let them go. Just as an athlete needs daily exercise, your mind also needs practice to eradicate the habit of judging. Your judgments of others and of yourself are hurting you. They fill you with guilt and make it impossible for you to forgive. Something to understand is that no one is judging you but yourself. Begin by observing everything in your life without judgment. You can do it. Try it.

It's worth it.

What is the meaning of prayer?

When I was a child we used to say several prayers before going to sleep. We were praying to the saints, the Holy Virgin, and especially the Christ child, Jesus. My mother used to read to us every night those prayers from a little booklet. I remember my two older sisters and I on top of her bed trying to do our best to concentrate. Sometimes we started to laugh while hoping my mother did not notice. Always, we were promptly reprimanded by her, saying were laughing because the "devil" got inside us.

The moment of asking for our wishes was our favorite part of the prayer. The other parts were so repetitive that we were able to say them without thinking, or we would simply think about something else. However, at the moment we were allowed to ask for something we needed, we were really focused and quiet, down on our knees with our palms joined together, our hands touching our little faces. I especially remember asking for my academic performance to improve, for the fighting to stop with my sisters, for my parents to cease fighting with each other as well, for the kid in my class to fall in love with me, and for us to have a more beautiful house. The "asking for your desires" was my favorite part, not just because I could ask; but because somehow I was allowed to talk directly with someone else, the one who had the power, (only if I was a good girl) to change my destiny and make me the happiest child in the world.

Paradoxically, while I was growing up I kept the same way of thinking, while at the same time, an unstoppable desire of "real communication" started burning within me. At some point in my life I did not want more "asking." I wanted answers. What I never would have imagined was all my prayers were always heard, and the answers were in a place that I never expected, inside of me. I then realized that most of the time I was bargaining for the outcome I wanted. I was not praying. I discovered that asking is not necessarily praying. To pray is to communicate. From time to time I used to offer a little something in order to "prove" I was serious in the negotiation. But do you really think I could bargain with God? He isn't interested in negotiating what is the most convenient thing for me. Eventually, I had to learn how to be humble and recognize that I didn't know my own best interest. How could I dare to tell God the way He has to act, or the things He has to do for me to be happy? Do I really have any clue about what I need to be happy? If I have no idea what is the best for me, what can I ask for? I could keep asking for things that did not have any value, and thus remain separate from my happiness.

By this process of thinking I learned two things. First, nothing in this world could bring me happiness in the way I was expecting. Second, God is always talking to me. He is always trying to communicate with me. My prayers became an opening of myself and my mind to receive what He has already given me. This was the recognition He already knows what is the best for me before I even ask.

My prayers became a listening to what He wants me to do without demanding, trusting, being still and letting Him lead the way. That is the miracle I have come to know as true prayer.

The decision between love and fear

Stories of forgiveness: Edward
His testimony

One quiet summer´s evening in the small Florida town of Blackstone Beach, an explosion rips through the night air. The Foundation for the Protection of Women had been attacked once again. This time the homemade bomb took out the front of the building. Most of its windows and some of its offices were destroyed.

Although unproven, the suspects involved were part of a gang, mostly made up of members of one family who had terrorized the area for years and who were also known to be involved with drugs and other local crimes.

In weeks previous to the explosion, the wife and daughter of the gang leader were relocated by the police with help of the Foundation to a safe house in another state. This attack was believed to be retribution by the gang

This wasn't the first time the Martinez family had been involved in such incidents. They had several complaints of robberies and were suspects in a local murder investigation. Even the police feared to approach them. However, three employees of the Foundation, Mary, Lisa and Edward, in a huge show of courage, went to the gang leader's house to ask them to pay for the damage to the facilities. As expected, they denied any responsibility and demanded evidence of these allegations. Lisa pointed to Edward, and said, "he saw the whole thing". This turned the rage of the gang members directly toward Edward. They didn't like the idea of having an eye-witness to their crimes.

One night, while Edward was alone in his home, he heard a car stop right in front of the house. He lived far from the city, and the nearest neighbor was at least two miles away. The young frightened man looked out the window and saw a parked car. It was the Martinez family, four of them, all dressed in black.

At that moment, recalled Edward, "I thought it was the end of my life. My friends were far away, and I had no phone to communicate with anyone, so I crawled into a corner of the room and began to pray."

"All I could do at that time was beg God for help. I started having one of the most incredible experiences of forgiveness, more wonderful than I ever thought possible."

I have no idea how long I stayed crouched in that corner, shaking; but suddenly I began to visualize the men, one by one in front of me, and I started talking with them in my mind. I could see every detail of each face, and I could feel what was inside their hearts. I saw a lot of fear and rage. I told each one from my heart that I understood their pain, for I was aware that no one had expressed love to them in their lives. In that moment I was able to see the love of God in them. I told them in my mind, if they intended to kill me, I would not go with resentment in my heart. On the contrary, the last words I would say to them would be, "I love you." The last thing I wanted them to hear out of my mouth would be an expression of love and forgiveness.

It was a very intense experience. I was completely soaked in sweat. When I finished telling this to each one of them in my mind, I heard the car engine suddenly start, and the gang drove off without even attempting to enter the house."

Months Later the gang had disbanded, some members were in prison and others left the neighborhood altogether. While in prison, two of them began a radical transformation in their lives. They became born again Christians and began a new life, free from the darkness of their past.

For many years Mary, Lisa and Edward continued to run the Foundation, helping victims of domestic violence. Edward has become a tireless social worker and public speaker, spreading the message of the healing power of forgiveness, in his home state of Florida and throughout the United States, helping thousands of individuals escape the bondage of domestic abuse..

The world I see holds nothing that I want.
Beyond this world there is a world I want. (ACIM)

Thank god?

Several years ago, during one of my usual walks to lunch, my colleague, Martin, posed an interesting question.

"I do not understand why I should say thank God," Martin exclaimed. "If the one that makes everything happen is me and not Him. If we have free will to do right or wrong, what does He have to do with it?

We both continued walking in silence. His argument did not resonate with me at all, and I did not how to respond. I had no answer to his question. Not until many years later could I understand what was going on in my friend's mind.

At the time Martin conceived of God as a man with a long beard sitting on a throne, someone who spent his time taking careful note of each of the faults of the mortals below. God was not exactly a fool or prone to overlook our sins. On the contrary, He had an angry temper and an excellent memory. He gave us free will. We can either do good works that would give us the right to enter to Heaven, or commit enough sins to throw us into eternal fire after we die. Meanwhile, we could be punished or rewarded on our way through this "valley of tears" we call life. That idea would reduce God to be the deliverer of rewards or punishments in our attempts at survival. That's why Martin could not thank him, he explained.

I was taught a similar definition of God from childhood; a description I considered correct, until I began to ask questions that no one could answer. However, amid this questioning I had my first revelation: only an experience could show me the essence of God.

Everything began to resolve in my mind when I could recognize his presence within me, and when I realized that He was not separate from us. This meant God was not a being who was sitting in a palace, pointing at us with an accusing finger. If He was inside me, He could have never forsaken me. Then came to my mind those painful memories when I thought I was alone. How much time I wasted, and how much pain I would have avoided if I had understood this from the beginning.

If God were a perfect being, and his love was immutable, He could not have any human characteristics like anger. I discovered that He was not waiting to punish me. The only one who had done that was myself, with my mistaken decisions. He loved me for no reason. His will for me had always been perfect happiness, nothing else.

So I began to remember...

Maybe I had a glimpse of His presence as a child

when I felt the fullness of the warmth of my parents or when I melted into the undisturbed peace of the sleep of my newborn nephews and nieces; perhaps when I gazed at the sunset, the fantastic brushstrokes in the sky like the perfect nuances of an artist that culminates with a sigh his work for the day. Perhaps it came in seeing the reflection of the stars in the ocean mixing on the horizon until I was breathless. Yes, I had evidence of the presence of love and the perfection of the mind of God. And, if I was part of him, I would also share the same eternal nature of each of his works and of the entire universe as well.

Suddenly, as if a veil had been drawn back before my eyes, I realized the impossibility of doing harm to anyone, not for fear of retaliation; but because now I could recognize the presence of God in each one and in myself. If I loved myself, I would love God and every one of his creations. Any act against them would be an act against my own being. Any action against my being would be an action against them. We are in no way separate from each other.

That was the moment I stopped hurting myself. That was the hour of my emancipation.

Now I know that He is in me and I in Him. I can tell you that He also is in you and you in Him. To give thanks to Him would be to give thanks to ourselves.

I do not know where you are, Martin, or if one day you will read this reflection. It doesn't really matter. I thank you, because to answer your question; I had to undertake a journey to the limits of my mind to find a glimmer of truth, a journey that perhaps someone, somewhere undertook along with me.

Which path should I take?

Have you ever been taken by surprise by life's circumstances, caught in a challenging situation just when you thought everything was perfect? Has there been a time when you finally felt you had overcome the problems of this world and established a comfortable existence, and then something completely disrupts your peaceful illusion? You may have begun to be shaken out of your comfort zone.

The so-called comfort zone is so misleading that you may not even realize you are living in it. It is a zone where you are hypnotized by a seductive call. It makes you think you live in a place where you are apparently comfortable and at peace. You seem to fit impeccably into a life that does not require much effort on your part. It is the result of all your beliefs, time and the resources you've invested. Superficially, this place contains all that you need, however, you know you live in constant discomfort, and you wish for something to happen to push you to take the step that you never dared take.

If you want to be pushed, it will happen. You will be rocked hard, and you will be forced to leave that treasured, but sticky place. When this happens you will not feel at ease. To leave the comfort zone is not pleasant at the beginning; but if you´re savvy enough, you will understand the game of your own ego. You know in order to get out of your comfort zone something drastic needs to happen, something that forces you to change; but at the same time, you want to end up with your head held high, blaming someone else for your discomfort. For example: It would be embarrassing to admit to the world that you boycotted your own well being by losing your job, or your marriage, or your house, or all of them at the same time. Although the truth is you are the cause of your own troubles, you look for another person on whom to shift the responsibility, and you easily find them.

So there you are, breathing frantically, with a cold sweat rolling down your forehead, watching the ones you blame for all your disasters. There it is, in that dark place in your mind, in the bottom of your devastation, where all around is darkness, you will see two paths. The first is the thorny path of blame and anger. The second is the one which invites you to take responsibility for what you are seeing. This one not only prevents you from blaming someone else, but will make you recognize that everyone was only playing the role that you had given them.

The first path will keep you in hell, the second will set you free. Which one to take is up to you.

The second path will lead you to the warm arms of forgiveness, where you will see a world free of guilt and you will realize your true purpose for being here.

"This is the only thing that you need do for vision, happiness, release from pain and the complete escape from sin, all to be given you. Say only this, but mean it with no reservations, for here the power salvation lies:

I am responsible for what I see. I choose the feelings I experience, and I decide upon the goal I would achieve. And everything that seems to happen to me I ask for, and receive as I have asked.

Deceive yourself no longer that you are helpless in the face of what is done to you. Acknowledge but that you have been mistaken, and all effects of your mistakes will disappear". *ACIM Chap. 21*

There is a light in you the world cannot perceive. And with its eyes you will not see this light, for you are blinded by the world. Yet you have eyes to see it. It is there for you to look upon. (ACIM)

Start by being happy

When I was sixteen years old, I read a definition of intelligence which would become my first spiritual opening. In a world where being smart is measured by academic achievement and intellectual skills, the author of, "Your Erroneous Zones," Wayne Dyer, stated that the intelligence of a person should be measured by his ability to be happy

In his own words expressed as follows: *"We have come to believe that someone who has more educational merit badges, who is a whiz at some form of scholastic discipline (math, science, a huge vocabulary, a memory for superfluous facts, a fast reader) is "intelligent." Yet mental hospitals are clogged with patients who have all of the properly lettered credentials, as well as many who don't. A truer barometer of intelligence is an effective, happy life, lived each day and each present moment of every day."*

The moment I read this paragraph, the full value I had given to academic happiness, relationship happiness and material achievements collapsed before

119

my eyes. For the first time, I felt like the blurred lens in my mind began to be corrected. After being myopic all my life, I had finally begun to see with the right glasses. Intuitively, I was understanding what some years later I would fully experience, the freedom to do what I love and live life in the continuous present moment. Sometime later, I watched a lecture on happiness in Barcelona. The speaker, who had gone through a very difficult economic period in his country, asked the audience what they would do if they lost their job. Participants were quick to answer in unison, "Get a new one!"

"What for?" The speaker replied

"To have money," said the audience

"What for?" The speaker again asked

"To be happy," replied the audience.

We overheard a sigh, mixed with smiles in the audience, because basically everyone knew that this was a lie they decided to believe; perhaps to mitigate some of their monotonous life, perhaps to feel less miserable. Indeed, those who were doing their jobs solely to earn money were quite far from being happy.

"So now," the speaker continued, "Let's start from the beginning...

What do you want?"

"To Be Happy!" they all answered.

"If you want to be happy, do what you love!" He insisted.

"If you do what you love, you will become an expert at it. Money will cease to be a goal. It will come easily as part of performing what you do with expertise and passion."

When enthusiasm and love for what you do moves your life, when you give and share fully of yourself, what you do becomes a joyful and healing experience. When we act out of love rather than fear, we grasp the meaning of freedom.

"There is a voice that speaks to you constantly. Remain in silence and there you will begin to hear it. That voice that seems a little whisper at first will intensify and you will hear it loud and clear. It comes from your heart. You can rely on it completely because that is where God lives, and he never is going to deceive you." (LESSON 49 ACIM)

I share my experience of finding freedom in the absence of fear. It disappears when I feel supported by our creative source, in releasing the ballast of a past that does not exist, and anxiety of an illusory future.

Happiness and peace of mind are states which can be accessed whenever we want, when we stop giving value to what we do not have, and decide to drop the dagger we are wielding against ourselves.

There is no need to go through a long process to understand this. We can do it instantly when we open our minds to the Here and Now.

Why not love yourself just the way you are?

Eleanor is a beautiful blonde girl with green eyes and a cute smile. Her hair is long with golden highlights. She is thin, but not very tall. She reminds me of one of those classic dancers, whose delicate movements create an invisible aura around them. Despite her beauty, she has not been very fortunate in her relationships. She is committed to reducing her weight through a diet which she has broken many times.

One day, while she and I were working together, she told me, with some guilt, that the day before she had eaten several different chocolate desserts. Her pulse was altered by the intake of sugar, but above all from the disappointment of her lack of willpower. I noticed some embarrassment on her face and in her eyes. She was expecting a word of encouragement on my part, but I had to leave in haste before we could talk about it.

On my way home, I was thinking about what I could tell her, or rather, what I could say to myself now that I know every experience I have is a message to myself.

The idea of "sacrifice" began to haunt my mind.

When I got home, I looked at the meaning of sacrifice in the dictionary. Among eight other definitions, I found this: "to surrender or give up, or permit injury or disadvantage to, for the sake of something else".

How could we get something good out of this? For my friend her diet was a sacrifice, something that she really did not want to do. When we tell ourselves to do something that makes us unhappy, something that we do with displeasure, even for a noble cause, we don't do it all the way. If we do it half way then we feel guilty. And if we feel guilty, unconsciously we will want to be punished. Thus, we start an endeavor whose objective is our failure. In that sense it is quite successful because the endeavor is built on the basis of wanting to hurt ourselves.

The next day I had a chance to talk with Eleanor.

"Why do you want stay on your diet?" I asked.

"To be thin," she replied.

"Why do you want to be thinner?" I insisted.

"To be more beautiful," she stated, as if it was obvious.

"And if you are more beautiful, what will happen?" I asked.

"I do not know ... I'll find the love of my life," replied the girl, a little ashamed of her own response.

But Eleanor has no need to be thinner to deserve

love. She needs to love herself. If we do not love ourselves, no matter what we do, we will live our life in uneasiness. We will then set up goals in order to sabotage our attempts to achieve them, ensuring we remain living in constant frustration. Inadvertently, we will seek relationships that will continue the permanence of our conflict.

I told my friend

"When you love yourself, you will not want to do anything against your own being. You will clearly recognize what heals you and what hurts you. You will stop overeating, or hurting yourself with destructive relationships."

She looked at me as if she had heard this for the first time in her life.

"When you love yourself, you accept that you are perfect as you are created," I said emphatically.

Eleanor reached out and hugged me.

I remembered my mother used to tell my father to make the "sacrifice" and stop drinking; but how could it be considered a sacrifice to stop doing something that is killing us? On the contrary, it would be a gift that we would offer our self. The gift of life!

The only "sacrifice" that God asks is the sacrifice of fear. You will now recognize that you are love itself. He loves you and you don't need to do anything to deserve His love.

How much do you need?

You will need as much as you think you need. You could store large amounts of silver and gold or dress with garments woven with golden threads and fine fabrics of satin and silk. You could use expensive jewelry to adorn yourself or use perfume from the most exotic flowers in the world; but none of this will be able to water the desert of your heart. It is difficult to explain why, despite all the luxuries you have, you keep finding yourself in an ocean of fear and desolation.

Despite your emptiness you desire to collect more.

If you do, you will never know when to stop. Perhaps you have placed the attainment of your happiness at the end of a long list of desires, behind your gold coins and crystal palaces, beyond the worshiping of your own ego. You think every time you make one of your desires come true, you advance closer to your happiness. However, none of this happens. In fact, you are now further away. Protecting what little you have achieved, you have sacrificed more, and the fear of losing everything attacks you voraciously, like a bird of prey that snatches away the little peace you thought you had gained.

You think you are condemned to continue your routine in order to get more of the same, more riches, more luxury and more fear. Only when you realize that this conviction is false will you understand that you do not have to store anything to be happy.

Take this example of a friend of mine from Colombia:

Veronica is an executive of a prestigious company in the city. She works, on average, twelve hours a day, and although her income is quite generous, she does not consider it enough. One day I found her in the coffee shop of the company where she works. The lines on her forehead accentuated her depressed mood, making her look older than she really was. She seemed worried about her work and a little sad at the same time. As we shared a coffee, I asked her if she had used the gift cards we received from a fancy local restaurant, or the additional prizes we won in a recent company promotion.

"No, impossible," she said. "I have no time. I have to work. That's my fate," she replied with a sigh.

Two weeks later I told her that my husband and I made a short trip to celebrate our anniversary. It was a very romantic town a few hours from the city in a rural destination. I asked if she knew the place.

"No, I've never been there. I have no time. I have to work ... maybe someday when I win the lottery." she replied once again.

"I don't think the probability of winning the lottery

is very high, and if it did happen, it would be far from being a guarantee of your happiness," I answered. She looked at me, a little surprised by my answer and said,

"But what can I do? I have to work to live?" Then I told her,

"Enjoy what you do and give everything to the joy of serving. If you can't do that, where you are right now, change jobs. Nothing material will ever be able to give you the happiness you expect, not even receiving a lot of money. When you are in harmony with yourself, your whole life is aligned, including your finances. How much you need will no longer be a monetary question, it will be a question concerning your mental and spiritual well being. Eventually, you realize that everything you need you already have inside you, right here and right now. At this very moment you could allow the return of joy into your life and value what is really worth valuing, that which is invisible to the eye."

She listened to everything I had to say patiently, as if she had understood for the first time. In that same moment, she received a call from a client and began to rush off hastily. As she reached the door, she turned her face toward me, and with a big smile said, "Thank you!"

The power of love: breaking the chain of hatred.

Trying to comprehend what is happening in this world on a daily basis goes beyond the scope of our rational understanding. Most of the news ▮ reporting the most barbaric actions of the human race, which seem aimed at achieving our own annihilation.

Throughout the history of humankind, past and present injustices have been able to surpass even the atrocities conceived of in the most insane minds, making it seemingly impossible to find a solution to the war and violence. We cannot seem to eliminate the thinking which is the birthplace of misery, hatred and revenge, the fuel of death and desolation. If, indeed, revenge could have been the remedy for the injustices of the world, we would be living in a paradise. Sadly we are far from living in one. Only when we break the cycle of hatred will real peace be manifest in the world.

How do we break the cycle of hatred? We must completely reverse the way we have thought so far. We have tried to fix the problem at the level of the problem, with the useless tools that this type of thinking offers us. Now we have to step out of the box and look up. If it is impossible to annihilate our enemy without annihilating ourselves, we can then choose to lay our anger aside. If we have believed that only weapons have power, let us try something different. There is a power capable of overcoming any man-made weapon. It is the only true power there is, the power of love.

When we take the first step away from the path of hatred, we are actually taking the first step toward the path of love. These two paths are only separated by a single thought. By healing our thoughts we start making a difference in the world. Therefore, the first step has to start in our minds, then a wonderful chain of events will follow. For example, Robert, who had struggled with his new manager for months, decided that "just for today" he would not hate or criticize him. His energy, then, was focused in doing something creative in his work. The adrenaline that was generated by the presence of his boss was focused to complete his assignments in record time. The results arising from a job well done were appreciated by his colleagues and his boss. With a friendly gesture on his part, he began to see everyone differently. Eventually, it was easier and easier to accept the presence of his boss, and they began to work together, harmoniously. After several years, Robert acknowledged that he only had feelings of gratitude and kindness in his heart for the manager and his family.

When you decide not to hate, loving becomes easy.

"The holiest of all places on earth is where an ancient hatred has become a present love."

(ACIM)

If you feel hatred toward someone, choose love. Think of him and wrap him with all your love and light. Allow yourself to melt into the universe along with your former enemies. Instead of cursing them, love them, and repeat to yourself, *"Let every voice but God's be still in me."*

"Can you imagine how beautiful those you forgive will look to you? In no fantasy have you ever seen anything so lovely. Nothing you see here, sleeping or waking, comes near to such loveliness. And nothing will you value like unto this, nor hold so dear. Nothing that you remember that made your heart sing with joy has ever brought you even a little part of the happiness this sight will bring you." (The Forgiven World ACIM).

The scent of flowers is their gift to you. The waves bow down before you, and the trees extend their arms to shield you from the heat, and lay their leaves before you on the ground that you may walk in softness, while the wind sinks to a whisper round your holy head. (ACIM)

An angel in my life.

When I was thirteen years old I was a victim of a traffic accident. The bus was I going to take recklessly stopped in the middle of the street to pick up passengers and then took off, leaving me in the middle of the road. Wanting to return to the sidewalk, I did not realize that another vehicle was coming right towards me.

In the next second, I was on the pavement, fully conscious and without any pain. I noticed that people were beginning to gather around me with amazement and worried faces. For a moment I thought I would get up and go home. However, when I saw my left foot, my hopes faded completely. My shoe was split open and my foot started to swell up as I had never seen before.

I was angry with myself for not having noticed the traffic. I was afraid of being scolded by my parents, and I was especially frustrated, thinking that what had happened would serve only as another traffic statistic in the city. Years later, I would discover that I had been wrong about all of this.

The driver of the car that hit me very nervously got out of his car. He picked me up, picked up my backpack and took me to a nearby hospital. I waited for two hours in a lonely hallway before being attended to. Noticing every detail of the white walls around me, I started to see in my foot turn shades of color from green to violet. I tried to get used to the strange swollen form that it had taken. It was impossible to hide my deformed toes. All I could do not to alarm my parents any further was to be as alert and as lucid as possible. After they examined me, doctors discovered a soft tissue injury. I had no fracture nor need of surgery. I just had to be still for the next month.

In those years, I had no means of communication with my parents. There were no cell phones, and the only phone number I knew was my grandparent's. So, the hospital staff, after they finished watching the soccer game, contacted them. Very soon my grandfather appeared, ready to take me home.

Since my family and I lived on the third floor of a building without an elevator, I had to climb the stairs, taking small leaps to get to my apartment, leaning on my 75 year old grandfather for assistance. In the middle of our climb, we stopped for a moment to catch a breath. When we were determined to continue. I pressed on, hopping only on my right foot. My older sister and Gloria, a new neighbor whom I had never met before, rushed over to help us. They could lift me up more easily together and bring me the rest of the way up the stairs.

Since my parents, who worked all day, could not take care of me, I had to stay in bed until my other sister got home from school to prepare lunch. By the time when my fifteen year old sister finished cooking, around 3 or 4 pm, my appetite was totally gone. I remember one day seeing her, angry and concerned, due to my complete inability to eat anything. This scene, curiously, was one of the first expressions of affection from her that remained registered in my memory.

Lying in bed, long before the days of cable TV, internet, tablets or mobile phones, my mornings were very long and lonely. All I could do was sleep and think. I easily started to get depressed and at times began to cry for no reason. During these days I lost weight very quickly.

One day, Gloria, the same neighbor who had helped me weeks earlier, asked my mother about my recovery. She inquired as to who fed me while they were absent. My mother, with much regret, let her know it was my sister who fed me when she came home from school. So Gloria asked for the keys to our apartment and promised to bring me a meal during the day. I was very grateful to know that now I wasn't only going to receive a delicious hot meal, but also some reading material as well. Now I could read and focus my mind on something other than my self-pity. I soon discovered the Reader's Digest and the interesting stories about people living in the winter, with deer and snow and salt-covered roads. All this for me, who was born in a tropical country, sounded like stories from another world. I was fascinated by this strange new land. A couple of decades later I would understand firsthand all of what these stories told.

With a new mind, my healing was accelerated. I

spent hours reading funny stories from a section of the magazine called, "Healing Through Laughter." With new energy running through my mind, my recovery became more noticeable. I became very skilled at hopping through the house from one place to another. Each personal breakthrough inspired me to get up and start a new one.

I was very young back then. I could never express my gratitude to Gloria the way I wanted to. She was the first person to show me that it is possible to perform a selfless act of love for perfect stranger.

I also thanked my sister for trying to take care of me, not knowing how to do it, and my grandfather for appearing at the time I needed him.

As I said at the beginning of this story, I had been wrong about everything. There really are no accidents. I was not a victim, because everything always has a purpose. The anger I felt against myself became self-forgiveness. All I could feel from my parents was their love and support, not their reproaches. But the most valuable thing was to understand that what happened that day was not to serve as another statistic in the city, but was to show me the true essence of my being. The selfless actions of Gloria and my family were demonstrations of love and compassion, the same which were taught by a humble man a little more than two thousand years ago.

The freedom of letting go

When I tried to escape the unhappiness I felt in life, nothing seemed to work.

After making several attempts, I realized that I could experience an increased release only if I started to abandon my obstinate ideas, rather than defending them. If I stopped clinging to my view of how to fix what I perceived as my problems, perhaps the most convenient solution would appear immediately.

Although I crashed several times against a wall, I held onto my attempts to solve everything my way. In each one of my failures, I could see parading before me all those responsible for my upsets: my parents, my colleagues, my partners. However, in none of the cases did my own image appear. Disheveled and sitting in a corner of my mind, I did not understand why I received such unpleasant results, if in fact, I was doing things so well. I deserved what I wanted and not what I was getting. Years later, I became convinced that the best outcome would not have been the one I wanted. In every case the solution had always been there, even before I invented the problem.

I had to put aside my arrogance, to recognize that most of the time I was unable to see what was best for me. The noise of my thoughts was so loud I could not realize the useless hours spent around imaginary drama. Nor did I see the ridiculous solutions that my pride offered me. On the contrary, I valued them with high esteem.

A new idea came to my mind. If by doing the same thing, I was getting the same result, I should do something new. If I stepped aside, and I did not insist on my old way of doing things, the real solution would appear. Thus, the action of letting go began to emerge in my life; initially as a timid experiment, which immediately became my first experience of freedom.

Gradually, this timid experiment turned into something more natural and stronger as I let go of my stubborn ideas. I could see that it would also be possible to release the resentments and guilt I had inflicted on myself for so long. Thus, I made letting go a constant practice in my life, remembering that "I don't know the purpose of anything," and then, listening to the one that knows.

No one was responsible for my afflictions, only my own thoughts.

Now I can...Release and listen, be still and know

Forgiveness showed me there is no death

Stories of forgiveness: Andrew
His testimony

My story begins more than eighteen years ago, at the time of my father's battle with cancer and apparent passing from this earth. The guilt I felt during that time was immense and total. I had been with a spiritual teacher for years and was already undergoing my own transformation. However, this was the first moment I really felt the total responsibility for my own reality. I was devastated by the guilt and the idea that my thoughts of separation were the cause my father's cancer. Yet the truth of it could be not escaped in my mind. During those days, I was also consumed by an emotional breakdown which was directly related to my father's illness and my fear and guilt. Where was the forgiveness of this dream, I asked constantly to God? How could this happen? Why now? Why him? I never had the chance to heal our relationship. I never told him how much I loved him. And he never let me in. I never asked him for forgiveness. Where will my healing come from? One of his last days in the hospital, I looked at my father lying there, with tubes in his arms, and suddenly I saw him whole and perfect. I knew he was going to leave his body soon, but I also had an immediate experience that death was impossible. I had to forgive myself for this seeming experience of Death.

It was then I began to remember all the love I had covered over in my mind with my judgments and grievances. Starting from that day there began a flood of memories from my life, as a deep appreciation of my father and my family grew inside of me.

I remembered a day at the beach when I was eleven years old. The time we went skating on the pond, my first baseball glove, all our times together on the golf course, even the smell of his cigarettes became beautiful memories of his love for me and my love for him. I tried to communicate all this to him when I looked into his eyes at the hospital. I couldn't tell him with my words; but I know in that moment he remembered as well all the love we had shared over the years.

About a year later, my mom told me of an incredible light experience she had with my Dad at the moment of his departure.

She described holding his hand and taking him to God and to Heaven, into a wonderful light. She felt an overwhelming peace in that moment. And when she opened her eyes, he was gone, and a beautiful warm light filled the room, and his presence was everywhere.

Sharing this story with her was one of my first

moments of the recognition that I was indeed only forgiving myself, that there is no death, and everyone is in Heaven right now. Sometimes, when I doubt this, my dad shows up for me, in a beautiful spiritual reminder that he is standing beside me in the light. He reminds me life is eternal and my forgiveness was felt by him that moment when our eyes locked in the hospital room. His presence reminds me we are together now and forever! Thanks dad!

I will not value what is valueless, and only what has value do I seek, for only that do I desire to find. (ACIM)